S. Hrg. 114–720

THE NORTH ATLANTIC TREATY ORGANIZATION, RUSSIA, AND EUROPEAN SECURITY

HEARING

BEFORE THE

COMMITTEE ON ARMED SERVICES
UNITED STATES SENATE

ONE HUNDRED FOURTEENTH CONGRESS

SECOND SESSION

THURSDAY, JULY 7, 2016

Printed for the use of the Committee on Armed Services

Available via the World Wide Web: http://www.fdsys.gov/

U.S. GOVERNMENT PUBLISHING OFFICE

27–770 PDF · WASHINGTON : 2017

COMMITTEE ON ARMED SERVICES

JOHN McCAIN, Arizona, *Chairman*

JAMES M. INHOFE, Oklahoma
JEFF SESSIONS, Alabama
ROGER F. WICKER, Mississippi
KELLY AYOTTE, New Hampshire
DEB FISCHER, Nebraska
TOM COTTON, Arkansas
MIKE ROUNDS, South Dakota
JONI ERNST, Iowa
THOM TILLIS, North Carolina
DAN SULLIVAN, Alaska
MIKE LEE, Utah
LINDSEY GRAHAM, South Carolina
TED CRUZ, Texas

JACK REED, Rhode Island
BILL NELSON, Florida
CLAIRE McCASKILL, Missouri
JOE MANCHIN III, West Virginia
JEANNE SHAHEEN, New Hampshire
KIRSTEN E. GILLIBRAND, New York
RICHARD BLUMENTHAL, Connecticut
JOE DONNELLY, Indiana
MAZIE K. HIRONO, Hawaii
TIM KAINE, Virginia
ANGUS S. KING, JR., Maine
MARTIN HEINRICH, New Mexico

CHRISTIAN D. BROSE, *Staff Director*
ELIZABETH L. KING, *Minority Staff Director*

(II)

CONTENTS

(III)

THE NORTH ATLANTIC TREATY ORGANIZATION, RUSSIA, AND EUROPEAN SECURITY

THURSDAY, JULY 7, 2016

U.S. SENATE,
COMMITTEE ON ARMED SERVICES,
Washington, DC.

The committee met, pursuant to notice, at 9:35 a.m. in Room SD–G50, Dirksen Senate Office Building, Senator John McCain (chairman) presiding.

Committee members present: Senators McCain, Inhofe, Sessions, Wicker, Ayotte, Fischer, Cotton, Rounds, Ernst, Tillis, Sullivan, Reed, Nelson, McCaskill, Manchin, Shaheen, Gillibrand, Blumenthal, Donnelly, Hirono, Kaine, King, and Heinrich.

OPENING STATEMENT OF SENATOR JOHN McCAIN, CHAIRMAN

Chairman McCAIN. Well, good morning. Senate Armed Services Committee meets this morning to receive testimony on the NATO [North Atlantic Treaty Organization] alliance, Russia, and European security.

We're grateful to our witnesses for appearing before the committee today: Ambassador Nicholas Burns, a distinguished member of the faculty at Harvard's Kennedy School of Government and former U.S. Permanent Representative to NATO; General James Jones, Chairman of the Scowcroft Center on International Security at the Atlantic Council—among many senior positions he held during his long career in public service, General Jones served as Supreme Allied Commander Europe for NATO and Commander of U.S. European Command; and Julianne Smith, Senior Fellow and Director of the Strategy and Statecraft Program at the Center for a New American Security and former Deputy National Security Advisor to Vice President Joe Biden.

Ambassador Burns and General Jones are the authors of the Atlantic Council's new report on "Restoring the Power and Purpose of the NATO alliance." Ms. Smith served as a member of the report's review board. I thank the Atlantic Council and all those that contributed to this timely, substantive report.

Last week marked the 100th anniversary of the start of the Battle of the Somme in World War I, 141 days of carnage that killed or wounded over one million soldiers. This is a powerful reminder of a time fading from memory, yet not all that distant, that Europe was a war-torn continent. It's also a reminder of how fortunate we are that the United States and our allies changed that tragic arc of history at a crucial inflection point. We forged the rules-based international order out of the ashes of World War II. We are committed, ourselves, to human rights, democracy, rule of law, open markets, and peaceful settlements of disputes, and we built a NATO alliance to protect, defend, and advance a Europe whole, free, and at peace.

Again we stand at a critical inflection point as the shadow of war is returned to Europe. The Atlantic Council report warns, and I quote, "The peace, security, and democratic stability of Europe can no longer be taken for granted." Today, the NATO alliance faces the greatest threat to peace and security in Europe since the end of the Cold War. Indeed, the challenges to our alliance are great: radical Islamic terrorism radiating instability across the Middle East, the worst refugee crisis since World War II, a weakened European Union, and perhaps most significant of all, a revanchist and unrepentant Russia willing to use military force to achieve political objectives.

Two years ago, for the first time in seven decades on the European continent, Vladimir Putin invaded and annexed the territory of a southern—of a sovereign nation by force. Unfortunately, since then he has learned from bloody experience in Ukraine, and now in Syria, that military adventurism pays, that diplomacy can be manipulated to serve his strategic ambitions, and that the worst refugee crisis since World War II can be weaponized to divide the West and weaken its resolve.

Two years later, our alliance is still struggling to adjust to the scope, scale, and seriousness of the new strategic reality we face. Confronted by brazen aggression, the Obama administration maintains its refusal to provide Ukraine with the lethal assistance it needs to defend itself. Many of our NATO allies have failed to reverse declining defense budgets and honor their pledge to reach the two percent target within a decade. Setting aside targets, the reality is that European defense spending is simply not commensurate with the security challenges faced by the alliance. Many NATO allies have inexplicably been reluctant to make the strategic investments in critical military capabilities needed to further alliance inoperability and improve readiness.

That said, there has been important progress. NATO has stood up a Rapid Reaction Force, increased air policing and sea patrols, expanded training and exercises, and moved more forces and equipment east toward the Baltic states, Poland, and the Black Sea region. Yet, it concerns me to hear senior European officials criticize even these limited steps to provide credible deterrence against Russian aggression as, "saber-rattling or warmongering." Such comments suggest a troubling head-in-the-sand mentality that yearns for a speedy return to the days of the delusional Russia reset and what General Breedlove has called "hugging the bear." Worse, such comments fundamentally misrepresent and undermine NATO's recent effort to defend itself. At a time of renewed danger, our alliance seeks to reaffirm and reinforce a decades-old commitment to promote a Europe whole, free, and at peace. That is what we must continue to do as we work to ensure the credibility of NATO's collective defense commitment in all domains: conventional, cyber, hybrid, and nuclear.

Finally, let me add that a strong NATO is in America's national security interests. Nowhere has that been made more clear than in Afghanistan, where our allies have sacrificed blood and treasure fighting alongside us for 15 years. Our shared mission is not over yet. That's why I welcome the President's announcement yesterday that the United States will retain 8,400 troops in Afghanistan into next year. I believe that conditions on the ground warranted retaining the current force level of 9,800. I fail to see any strategic rationale for the withdrawal of 1,400 U.S. troops while the security situation remains, in the President's own word, "precarious."

That said, it's important the United States signaled our ongoing commitment to the mission in Afghanistan ahead of the NATO summit in Warsaw, this week, where our allies will make troop and funding commitments to the Resolute Support mission. I believe the commitments our allies make this week will once again demonstrate that NATO is a critical force multiplier and a vital partner to promote global stability and security.

I look forward to hearing from our witnesses today, and the opportunity to discuss their recommendations for strengthening the NATO alliance, reinvigorating U.S. global leadership, and meeting our shared challenges.

Senator Reed.

STATEMENT OF SENATOR JACK REED

Senator REED. Well, thank you very much, Mr. Chairman.

Let me join you in welcoming the witnesses, thanking them not only for their testimony today, but for their service to the Nation in so many different ways.

Thank you very, very much.

The NATO alliance and our partners are confronted by a security landscape that has undergone drastic changes in recent years. NATO faces multiple threats to regional stability, including ongoing Russian provocations in the east which flout international norms; the conflicts in Syria, Iraq, and North Africa which continue to destabilize the region and have driven a historic number of refugees to flee into NATO countries; and the prospect that radicalized citizens of NATO countries may export their battlefield training from these conflicts in the Middle East back to their home country. In addition, there are challenges beyond the military domain, in areas such as economic stability, in cyber and energy security. When the NATO summit begins in Warsaw tomorrow, all of these issues will be discussed at length.

Two years ago, at the Wales summit, members agreed to several important steps in an effort to recalibrate the alliance with the new security environment. They approved a Readiness Action Plan to enhance the alliance's ability to respond quickly to security challenges. They affirmed defense spending commitments of two percent of GDP [gross domestic product], and agreed that it is not enough just to increase spending; investments must also be focused on strategic capabilities that strengthen the alliance. In Warsaw, expected announcements included enhanced forward presence to the east, the declaration of cyber as a domain, and the affirmation of NATO allies' and partners' long-term commitment to Afghanistan.

On that last point, I support the President's decision to retain approximately 8,400 United States troops in Afghanistan into 2017 to continue training, advising, and assisting the Afghan Security Forces and conducting counterterrorism operations.

Yesterday's announcement comes at an important time in this year's fighting season. It takes into account the advice of the commanders on the ground and gives clarity to our NATO allies as their own contributions are discussed at Warsaw this week.

The issue of deterrence, and what constitutes an effective deterrence, will also be discussed in Warsaw. Included in this year's Senate-passed National Defense Authorization bill is $3.4 billion for the European Reassurance Initiative, a fourfold increase over last year's funding. This funding is intended to enhance the U.S. military presence and activities in Europe and focus United States efforts more intently on deterrence measures. In addition, NATO will announce the deployment of four battalions to Estonia, Latvia, Lithuania, and Poland to enhance forward presence. As both of these initiatives move forward, it will be essential to ensure that they are integrated so that deterrence measures are amplified and not simply duplicated. I will be interested to hear our panelists' views on how best to—these integration efforts.

Thank you again, to our panelists, for their willingness to appear this morning. I look forward to your testimony.

Thank you, Mr. Chairman.

Chairman MCCAIN. I thank the witnesses. I do believe that this hearing is a very timely one, given the President and Secretary of Defense's departure for Warsaw for a NATO summit. I thank the witnesses.

Ms. Smith, we'll begin with you.

STATEMENT OF JULIANNE SMITH, SENIOR FELLOW AND DIRECTOR, STRATEGY AND STATECRAFT PROGRAM, CENTER FOR A NEW AMERICAN SECURITY, FORMER DEPUTY NATIONAL SECURITY ADVISOR TO VICE PRESIDENT JOE BIDEN

Ms. SMITH. Thank you very much. Thank you, Chairman McCain, Ranking Member Reed, and members of the committee, for the opportunity to testify this morning on the NATO alliance, on Russia, on European security.

As you both noted, the summit, the NATO summit, will start tomorrow in Warsaw, Poland, and run over two days. As you also know, NATO summits tend not to garner much attention by publics on the other side of the Atlantic or even by our public here in the United States. To the extent that Americans and Europeans notice that a summit's even occurring, what do they see? They see red carpets. They see handshaking. They see a lot of champagne toasts. They have a hard time understanding how all of that will have any impact on their day-to-day lives.

To the extent that they follow the details of the summit, or have in the past, they also hear lots of pledges by our European allies to spend more on defense. That has not happened over several decades, and they've seen those pledges essentially gone unfulfilled. But, I believe that this particular summit in Warsaw, the one that starts tomorrow, is worth watching and deserves a considerable amount of praise. Let me take just a few minutes to explain why.

In terms of the actual deliverables at the summit, the first deliverable is the fact that we're having a summit at all. The summit is one of the deliverables. What do I mean by that? Well, with Europe buckling under the weight of Brexit, the migration crisis, counterterrorism challenges, instability in the Middle East, and a resurgent Russia, this summit is a very useful and, Senator McCain, you used the word, "timely" opportunity for the transatlantic partners to come together and showcase resolve, solidarity, and unity at a time when, frankly, they need it most.

In regards to the threats that NATO faces east, we've already heard some of the ways in which the alliance is going to be strengthening its policies and tools to address those threats. Most notably in the area of deterrence, the alliance will be adding four new multinational brigades—battalions, I'm sorry—in the three Baltic states and Poland.

In regards to the threats that NATO faces in the south, the alliance will be making two major decisions. One, it's going to increase training and capacity-building inside Iraq, which is rare for the alliance. The alliance tends to prefer to do those types of things outside of conflict zones. This is an important decision. The alliance is going to assume the risk and take on these types of missions inside Iraq.

Two, the alliance is going to announce that it's going to be deploying AWACS [Airborne Warning and Control System] as part of the anti-ISIS [Islamic State of Iraq and Syria] coalition, which is also important, because, frankly, I think the alliance has been trying to avoid getting involved in this conflict for quite some time.

As another deliverable, I would note that the alliance is taking the rather controversial decision of adding Montenegro, its 29th member, to the alliance. This is obviously important news for Montenegro, which has worked tirelessly to meet all of the criteria for NATO membership, but, more importantly, this is a way that the West can send a very strong signal to Moscow that sovereign nations have the right to determine freely, or choose freely, their associations and alliances.

There will be other important initiatives at this summit announced over the next two days, and we can get into those details perhaps later this morning, but, just quickly, I would note that the alliance will be reaffirming NATO nuclear policy. This is something, frankly, that the alliance has almost forgotten about in recent years. That will be put back on the agenda. You'll also see some new initiatives in regards to EU [European Union]/NATO cooperation, which is important, because these are two institutions that have been unable to cooperate over several decades. You'll hear more about resilience and ways in which the alliance is going to be strengthening the toolkit it has to respond to the hybrid tactics that our friends in Russia are using. You'll hear some news—not enough good news, but some good news—on defense spending, as well.

But, ultimately, we have to ask ourselves, Is all of this enough? I would answer no. After the red carpets are rolled up, after all those handshakes and the champagne toasts and the praise that NATO deserves for this summit, NATO has to get back to work. In particular, I think the alliance needs to turn its attention to

Libya, which is now commonly described as the second-biggest source of instability in the Euro-Atlantic area, after Syria. I think the alliance is going to have to ensure that those new battalions are reinforced and can be sustained over the long term. The alliance is going to have to focus on defense spending and ensure that allies are continuing to march towards that two percent target. We're also going to have to spend some time on Romania and Bulgaria and the Black Sea, a region that has received less attention than the Baltic states. Finally, we're going to have to look at what other tools NATO can develop in cooperation and working with the EU to deal with cyberthreats, strategic communications challenges from the Russians, and all sorts of other hybrid tactics that they regularly use. Above all, we have to ensure that NATO can continue to rely on U.S. leadership, which has been a key ingredient to the alliance's success over many, many decades.

In closing, I'd only state that I disagree with those that say NATO is obsolete. It is imperfect, but it is also capable of innovation, adaptation, and concrete policy initiatives that make a real difference in enhancing European security and our own security. We'll see plenty of evidence of that over the next two days.

Again, thank you very much for the opportunity. I look forward to your question.

[The prepared statement of Ms. Smith follows:]

July 7, 2016

Testimony before the Senate Armed Services Committee
"The North Atlantic Treaty Organization, Russia, and European Security"

Julianne Smith, Senior Fellow and Director, Strategy and Statecraft Program
Center for a New American Security

Chairman McCain, Ranking Member Reed, and members of this committee, I greatly appreciate the opportunity to testify today in advance of the NATO Summit, which will take place in Warsaw on July 8th and 9th. Often to the dismay of the policymakers that spend months of their lives preparing for them, such summits rarely garner much attention on either side of the Atlantic. To the extent that NATO summits are covered in the media, one sees lots of red carpets, hand shaking, and champagne toasts. For the general public, it is often hard to see how such a large gathering of world leaders signing communiques with promises of "transformation" and "smart defense" will have any real impact on their daily lives. Even NATO experts sometimes find the summits disappointing, especially the countless pledges to increase defense spending that have been met for years with inaction. This year's NATO summit in Warsaw, though, will be an entirely different affair both in substance and style. The Alliance is about to demonstrate that it is anything but obsolete.

The Warsaw Summit comes at a precarious time for the transatlantic relationship. It will occur exactly two weeks after the UK's shattering decision to leave the European Union (EU) and a little more than a week after the suicide bombings in Turkey. The Summit will therefore be an opportunity for the transatlantic partners to showcase solidarity, unity, and resolve at a time when they need it most. As a NATO-nik, I am usually reluctant to give NATO members credit just for showing up. Instead, I prefer to judge summits based on their "deliverables" or concrete policy changes. But this year is different. With the entire European project buckling under the weight of Brexit, the historic migration crisis, counter terrorism challenges, a resurgent Russia, and instability close to Europe's borders, one of the deliverables is simply the Summit itself. If Brexit has taught us anything, it is that we should not take the liberal order for granted. Holding the NATO Summit now serves as a timely reminder of the values we share and the bonds that keep us together, particularly in the face of so much adversity.

More importantly, the Warsaw Summit will feature policy changes that will bolster the Alliance's ability to tackle threats to its east and south. After its last summit in Wales in 2014, some members criticized the Alliance for failing to do more to deter Russian aggression. NATO heard those complaints and spent much of last year looking at ways it could increase its deterrence measures. It wasn't easy. Due to geographic, cultural, and historical differences, members hold widely disparate views on Russia and have had a hard time determining the right balance between prudent planning

and needless escalation. But in a surprising twist, the Alliance has decided to deploy four multinational battalions to the Baltic States and Poland. That is a bold move for an alliance that tends to err on the side of caution. In fact, combined with what the U.S. is doing unilaterally in the region, it is the largest gathering of combat power in one area since the Cold War.

In Warsaw NATO will also announce ways in which it will do more to address instability across the Middle East. After considerable debate about the risks involved, the Alliance will agree to a training and capacity building effort *inside* Iraq alongside its current efforts in Jordan. To fully appreciate why such an announcement is newsworthy, one needs to understand that while NATO has considerable experience in training foreign forces, it prefers to do that training away from conflict zones. By taking steps toward doing more inside Iraq, the Alliance is demonstrating a willingness to assume more risk in order to increase the speed and effectiveness of its training programs. The Alliance has also decided to deploy AWACS as part of the anti-ISIS campaign. These surveillance aircraft will play a helpful role in a conflict that the Alliance has up until now been trying to avoid.

In addition to addressing the threats to its east and south, NATO will take the controversial step of welcoming Montenegro as a new member. Why, one might ask, is adding such a small country so controversial? Some members oppose enlargement for fear of escalating already high tensions with Moscow. Others argue that the Alliance should focus on its core mission of collective defense and that adding another member now would only complicate efforts to do so. The Alliance managed to work through such objections and in the end, opted to send a clear signal that sovereign nations have the right to freely choose their security arrangements and alliances.

The list of policy changes at this summit will not stop there. Expect to hear a lot about "resilience" and how NATO and the European Union will do more together to finally break through years of paralysis to address Russian hybrid tactics. Expect to hear that two-thirds of Alliance members have finally stopped the bleeding when it comes to their national defense budgets after years of budget cuts. Expect to hear a few words about NATO's nuclear policy; a subject the Alliance has almost forgotten in recent years. It will now reaffirm and update that policy in response to Putin's nuclear saber rattling.

Are all of these initiatives are enough? Certainly not. After Warsaw, after the champagne toasts, after the speeches and policy announcements, the Alliance will have to get back to work. Despite all of its good work since its last summit in 2014, the Alliance will continue to face a number of compounding security challenges that will require more debates, innovation and investment. Specifically, NATO – with a heavy dose of U.S. leadership – will need to:

- Do more to address instability in Libya, which is now commonly described as the second biggest source of instability in the Euro-Atlantic neighborhood after Syria.
- Ensure its new battalions in the Baltic States are reinforced.
- Push its members to do more to address readiness gaps. Larger allies should be prepared to

deploy a brigade on 10-day readiness and smaller allies should provide battalions on 10-day readiness

- Focus on Russian anti-access, area denial (A2/AD) challenges in and around Romania and Bulgaria.
- Ensure that the UK's departure from the European Union does not have a detrimental effect on UK defense spending or its role in NATO.
- Strengthen its capabilities and policies for addressing a wide range of threats and challenges to its south.
- Push more allies to move closer to the NATO target of spending two percent of GDP on defense.
- Strengthen the Alliance's relationships with countries like Sweden and Finland, a recommendation from the Center for a New American Security's (CNAS) table top exercise "Assured Resolve" that I ran with my colleagues this past February.

This list of future work shouldn't preclude us from saluting NATO's many achievements in recent months. Despite claims that it is outdated, ill-equipped for today's challenges, or entirely obsolete, this summit will showcase an alliance capable of self-reflection, rigorous debate, innovation, adaptation, and concrete policy changes that strengthen European security.

Chairman McCain. Thank you.
Ambassador Burns.

STATEMENT OF HONORABLE R. NICHOLAS BURNS, GOODMAN PROFESSOR OF DIPLOMACY AND INTERNATIONAL RELATIONS, HARVARD KENNEDY SCHOOL

Ambassador Burns. Thank you, Mr. Chairman, Senator Reed, members of the committee. Thank you for the opportunity to testify this morning.

Twenty-five years ago this autumn, we in NATO believed that Europe's historic demons of war and division—and you referenced them this morning, Mr. Chairman, in your statement—we thought they had been vanquished, because communism collapsed, Germany was united in NATO, the United—the USSR vanished from the scene, and that allowed President George H. W. Bush to proclaim a strategic imperative that I think all administrations since, Democrat and Republican, have agreed on, that Europe is whole, free, and at peace. It was one of the most significant foreign policy accomplishments in our history.

Twenty-five years later, General Jones and I believe that Europe and the United States are facing the greatest threat to the peace since the end of the Cold War. Specifically, we're encountering a dramatically changed and perilous security environment in Europe produced by four interlocking challenges. The first is Vladimir Putin's aggression, his division of Georgia and of Ukraine, his annexation of Crimea, his threats to the Baltic states, and his military's harassment of United States military forces in international airspace and international waters. The second challenge is a dramatically weakening and potentially fractured European Union, now exacerbated by the possible departure of the United Kingdom. The third is the tsunami of violence spreading from the Levant in North Africa into Europe, itself. The fourth is uncertain and sometimes seemingly unconfident European and American leadership in the face of these combined challenges.

It would be an exaggeration to say that we're returning to the Cold War or that our dream of a united, peaceful Europe is no longer attainable, but these are daunting risks requiring a rededication to one of our most enduring bipartisan objectives, a secure, durable, strengthened American link to Europe's future and Europe's success. That is why the NATO alliance remains so important to the United States. That is why such a changed security situation requires a significant and bold response by the United States and its NATO allies to Putin and the other threats that we mentioned.

The Atlantic Council report that General Jones and I shared makes many recommendations. You've seen them. But, the principal recommendation is that NATO should station military forces, on a permanent basis, in the Baltic states, in Poland, in the Black Sea region, and to have stronger capacity in the Arctic region. This will make NATO's strategic deterrence and our article 5 commitment to our allies real and unambiguous and unyielding to the Russian Government. It's the best way to secure the peace in Europe.

We may need to hold the line against Putin in eastern Europe for some time to come, and that is why we must also maintain American, European, and Canadian sanctions against Putin until he has met all the conditions of the two Minsk agreements negotiated with the Ukrainian Government, the British, and the French. To let him off the hook, as some European leaders are already advocating, would let him get away with larceny and aggression not seen in Europe—and you referenced this, as well, Mr. Chairman—in 70 years. That is also why the United States should extent lethal military assistance to Ukraine, so that it has the capacity to defend itself against clear and open Russian aggression.

We need, furthermore, to push our NATO allies to rebuild their militaries and spend much more in the—on the—on their defense, given this altered strategic environment. It is unacceptable that these wealthy countries are nearly all punching below their weight. Only five of the 28 NATO allies are spending above NATO's minimum of two percent of GDP on their national defense. We need, especially, a stronger Germany to help lead NATO, and help the United States lead NATO, in this new era. We need a stronger United Kingdom, France, Italy, Spain, and Poland, to enable NATO meet these new threats.

My final point, Mr. Chairman, is that our most complex challenge may come from within the NATO countries, themselves. Our strongest link, of course, is that we are all democracies, but many of us, including our own country, are confronting a wave of isolationist sentiment and, in some cases, extremism, in our domestic political debates. NATO is going to need strong, unflinching American leadership to cope with these challenges. The next American President will have the opportunity, and the obligation, to provide such leadership to weather these storms.

An early NATO Summit in 2017 could confirm the decision to keep adequate forces in Afghanistan, to train the militaries of Iraq and Tunisia and Jordan, to increase our national defense budgets, to maintain the sanctions on Putin, and to provide effective strategic deterrence against him. Most importantly, the next President must win the battle for public support here at home, within the United States. That effort should focus on what we know to be true, that our alliances strengthen, and they don't weaken, us; that American isolation, on the left and the right, is not the answer to these problems; and that NATO remains not only relevant, as Julie has said, but essential in this changed world where American leadership is so critical and so much in demand.

Thank you very much.

Chairman MCCAIN. General Jones.

STATEMENT OF GENERAL JAMES L. JONES, USMC (RET.), CHAIRMAN, BRENT SCOWCROFT CENTER ON INTERNATIONAL SECURITY, ATLANTIC COUNCIL, AND FORMER NATIONAL SECURITY ADVISOR

General JONES. Mr. Chairman, Senator Reed, members of the committee, thank you very much for inviting me to testify, along with my colleagues, before this committee on the important topic of NATO, Russia, and European security in the context of the upcoming NATO Summit in Warsaw.

I'm honored to work with the Atlantic Council and my friend—my friends, Ambassador Burns and Julianne Smith, in producing the study "Restoring the Power and Purpose of the NATO Alliance." We're pleased to submit this report as the official testimony for the record.

If you—with your permission, I'd like to make a few key points in reference to the major challenges facing the alliance and the way ahead. But, before I do, however, I'd like to make a reference to an issue about which I testified before this committee last year, and that's the deplorable treatment of refugees of Camp Liberty in Iraq.

On Monday, July 4th of this year, at 20:35 local time, the MEK [Mujahadeen-e-Khalq] at Camp Liberty came under the direct fire of 50 missiles and rockets launched by paramilitary forces associated with Iran's Quds Force and with the tacit approval of the Iraqi Government. This—attacks inflicted severe damage upon the residents of the camp, and a number of residents were severely injured, about 50. The MEK is continually subjected—is—has been continually subjected to attacks directed by the Iranian regime since their installation at Camp Ashraf. Monday's attack is the latest in an ongoing string of assaults on the residents at their current residence of Camp Liberty. All told, the MEK has been victim to eight attacks and have resulted in 140 people killed and over 1400 injured. It's only a matter of time, as I said last year, until they come under assault once again.

I previously recommended in testimony that the United States Government should adopt a much more compassionate view of the MEK and, by extension, a more aggressive posture when it comes to ensuring their safety. The United States Government took on an explicit obligation in 2003 to protect them while in residence, and now, I submit, in captivity, at Camp Liberty. To date, the—we have failed them miserably and tragically. Fourteen-hundred remaining members of this group are waiting to go to Albania today.

I'd also like to acknowledge the role of the Albanian Government in agreeing to accept the residents, and encourage the United States Government to do all it can to ensure the residents' swift and complete transfer to Albanian soil.

Mr. Chairman, the world and Europe face deep instability, the likes of which we have not seen in decades, which impacts our interests and the interests of our allies. Instability is the implacable enemy of peace and development, and directly threatens the interests of the United States and our allies. Europe faces the alarming prospect of real retreat and unraveling as—and, as we point out in this report, NATO faces its greatest security threats since the end of the Cold War.

There is today a—clear differences, in my view, in how the eastern European nations and the western European nations view the Russian threat. This undercuts a longstanding bipartisan United States goal of a united Europe whole and free. The security order in the Middle East is unraveling, which affects not only the Middle East, but also the United States and our allies in Europe. Sixty-five million people are now displaced by instability, perhaps the most in history. The move of migration towards Europe has deeply destabilized our European allies, and Africa could be right behind.

Retreat and isolationism from the world, however, do not suit U.S. interests or enhance American security, prosperity, and our values. In a world of rising instability, U.S.-led alliances enhances our security, bolsters global stability, and enhances U.S. influence globally. Vacuums are created when leadership—U.S. leadership is not present and is not visible.

The first point I'd like to make is that NATO is a force multiplier for United States, not a burden. Our 27 NATO allies offer American forward basing, which allows us to better fight enemies, like ISIS, and deter adversaries, like the new Russia, and to meet shared challenges. Twenty-eight countries acting as one is a powerful alliance.

Allies are instrumental to global security and have helped carry the security burden in places like Iraq and Afghanistan. Nearly 1,000 European and Canadian troops paid the ultimate price in Afghanistan. Our allies support us politically at the U.N. [United Nations] and through other political and economic organizations and coalitions.

NATO is also an anchor of stability. That is priceless in a world of instability. History clearly shows it is far less costly in blood and treasure to invest in maintaining Europe's peace than coming to Europeans' rescue after the outbreak of conflict, as we did in World War I and World War II.

There is a need for greater U.S. leadership in NATO. Over the last two administrations, the U.S. has retreated considerably from its historic leadership role within the alliance. It started in the Bush administration, and continues today. NATO functions best when the United States provides leadership. But, what does U.S. leadership mean? It means American officials make the case for NATO and do not denigrate our allies. Some are questioning the relevance of our most important security alliance, which is NATO. That's not vision and leadership. It's blindness and abdication, and it places America at risk. We must rally our allies to meet the most urgent threats at the doorstep: ISIL [Islamic State of Iraq and the Levant], Russia, refugees, the radical spread of fundamentalism, and the like. But, we must also position the alliance to address emerging threats before they become emergencies. This will require a new type of NATO. American leadership is important to convince our allies to take on a greater share of the security burden. We have a right to expect that our allies should do more, or at least to live up to their commitments that they've previously made, such as the two percent for—of their GDP [gross domestic product] for defense spending, agreed upon in 2002 at the Prague summit.

In a world of instability and hybrid threats, the United States must put forward a vision for a proactive NATO. NATO cannot be reactive in the 21st century. NATO should be active in forming partnerships and building security capacity in Africa and the Middle East. We need a stronger NATO/EU [European Union] relationship in the face of terrorists and hybrid threats. There is a need for NATO to take measures to enhance societal resilience, and NATO should consider how nonmilitary measures can affect security—for example, sanctions—and serve as important tools for influence, like energy security and cybersecurity, as well.

Mr. Chairman, the North Atlantic Treaty Organization is in a state of flux, but I'm confident that, with American leadership and persuasion, that, when you look at the world that we face, that we can shape this alliance, and we can make it—we can transform it into a 21st-century reality that will enhance our collective security.

Thank you.

Chairman McCAIN. Thank you, General. Thank you for bringing this—to the attention of the committee this latest attack on Camp Liberty. It is a compelling argument to get those people out of there as quickly as possible. Clearly we have failed in our commitment to them.

We need to get your opinion, the three witnesses, on the President's decision, instead of withdrawing down to what was once described as embassy-centric forces, where now the President has decided to have 8,400 troops remaining in Afghanistan. I don't see the rationale for withdrawing 1,400. I know for a fact that the military advice was to maintain 9,800. But, it's better than the—what had been planned and stated plans by the President.

We'll begin with you, Ms. Smith, on this latest iteration of our commitment in Afghanistan.

Ms. SMITH. Thank you, Mr. Chairman.

I support the decision to maintain higher troop levels inside Afghanistan. I am also in support of your personal view, that that number should be as high as possible and reflect the advice of our military commanders.

I look at it through an allied lens. I know from past experience, in my position working NATO issues inside the Pentagon, that, should the United States decide to leave, we would then see a rapid departure of all of our allies. The truth of the matter is that they have sacrificed a great deal and contributed considerably to the Afghan mission through many, many years; but the reality is that they cannot make those contributions without the support of the United States, without our enablers, the lift we provide, the medevac, the list goes on and on. So, I am glad to see that the number will stay higher than inspected. I wish it were a little higher. But, I am also glad because of the impact it will have on our allies that are on the ground with us in Afghanistan.

Chairman McCAIN. Ambassador Burns.

Ambassador BURNS. Mr. Chairman, I agree. I support the President's decision, but I also agree with you and Julie Smith that it would have been preferable to keep the number where the military wanted the number, at 9800. I was at NATO headquarters, visiting, ten days ago, and it was clear, in my conversations with the Secretary General and others, that NATO wants to stay, but they need the United States to stay and to lead. This will allow NATO to stay.

I would just conclude by saying that General Jones and I were both at NATO—Jim, as SACEUR [Supreme Allied Commander Europe], and I was Ambassador—when we deployed NATO to Afghanistan in August 2003. We didn't realize how long a mission it would be. But, looking at the security situation and the threat from the Taliban, al Qaeda, and the Islamic State in Afghanistan, and looking at, I think, some of the good measures of the current Afghan Government, we have an obligation to stay and help them succeed.

Chairman MCCAIN. Additionally, General Jones, as you know, in June there was a change in the rules of engagement, which previously had prohibited attacks on the Taliban, which is beyond bizarre. But, I'm glad that we have, now, that capability. Your comment?

General JONES. Mr. Chairman, I support the recommendations of the Chairman of the Joint Chiefs and the combatant commanders and the whatever. I do not know what they recommended, but I—I'm glad to see we're leaving a substantive force there.

I do think that President Ghani deserves our support. I think he has the right intellectual and sense of mission, in terms of what needs to be achieved in Afghanistan. The military piece is one, for sure, but the other is to do everything we can to help jumpstart the economy and show the Afghan people that there is a better future for them and their children. I think the third element is, obviously, governance and rule of law that the Afghan people need to see is moving in the right direction. So, it's—combination of those three things that I think will turn Afghanistan in the right direction.

All of us are continuously, for years, disappointed that our NATO allies haven't reached their two percent target, but it's also a myth that it continues to be conveyed that the U.S. accounts for about three-fourths of NATO funding. But, the Washington Post pointed out, on 30 March, that U.S. contributes 22 percent.

So, I guess my question, beginning you—again with you, Ms. Smith, is that—Mr. Trump has said, "NATO is obsolete. It's extremely expensive for the United States." Do you believe that NATO is obsolete? Obviously the—could you say, briefly, the consequences of our withdrawing for NATO or a dissolution of NATO?

Ms. SMITH. I'm not someone who believes that the alliance is obsolete. I think it has its flaws, and I think defense spending will continue to be a challenge. I would note that in 2015, last year, 16 allies spent more on defense than they had the year prior, and next year 20 of the 29 allies will spend more. Is it enough? No, it's not enough. We need to keep pushing them towards two percent. I would note that some allies, though, spend less than two percent, countries like Norway that contribute a great deal to the missions that we conduct around the world.

What would happen if the U.S. left the alliance? I think it would collapse. I think U.S. leadership is absolutely critical. I think this alliance serves our interests. It gives us very capable partners that have assets, that have capabilities, that have the will to act. They stand shoulder-to-shoulder with the United States to face aggression to the alliance's east, to its south. I think, particularly in light of Brexit, assuming it happens, the NATO alliance will be more important than ever.

Ambassador BURNS. Mr. Chairman, I think the United States provides 22 percent of the direct costs of NATO, as that Washington Post report indicated. There's a second figure. The United States defense spending is about 73 percent of all defense spending in Europe. So, there are different ways of looking at this. But, direct cost to Europe is 22 percent.

The key country in the debate about burden-sharing is going to be Germany. Chancellor Merkel, who I think has been a great leader and a great friend of the United States, said, last Wednesday, that she hoped Germany would be able to get to two percent. It was the most significant statement that we've heard from a German leader recently. She's not getting much help from her coalition partners, but, if she can be returned—and we don't know if that's to be the case—if Germany could step up—in the recent trends that Julie Smith has indicated, 20 of the allies have increased—have at least stopped cutting, and have modest increases. We need to push the Europeans in that direction.

Chairman McCAIN. So, you don't believe that NATO is obsolete?

Ambassador BURNS. I do not believe that NATO is obsolete, Mr. Chairman. I would say this. I think that Mr. Trump's comments, his consistent denigration of NATO and his consistent praise of Vladimir Putin, are completely misguided. I think he's already done a lot of damage to the alliance in threatening, implicitly, to walk out, by saying that NATO is obsolete and we shouldn't commit ourselves to it. I—the number-one strategic advantage we have over Russia and China is that we have alliances in Europe and Asia, and the Russians and Chinese do not. So, we should build those alliances.

Chairman McCAIN. General Jones?

General JONES. Mr. Chairman, I don't believe NATO is obsolete, but I do think it has been neglected a little bit in the—as I've mentioned in my remarks, that the absence of dedicated, visible leadership by the United States is absolutely essential to make a 28-country alliance work.

For example, in the aftermath of Russia's invasion of Crimea, in portions of the Ukraine, there was no emergency meeting of the North Atlantic Council [NAC] called for by the United States. I find that to be incredible. That is clearly in the backyard of the alliance. I think there should have been an emergency meeting of the NAC, as would—you would have expected during the Cold War.

Many NATO nations are participating in the NATO ISIL coalition in meaningful ways, but, as of now, the mission is taken through a U.S.-led coalition, and there's disagreement in the alliance about whether NATO should adopt a more formal role. I believe NATO should first develop a strategy for combating ISIL. NATO taking over command and control of the coalition will be much more effective—a much more effective use of resources. But, some allies may resist this move, for various reasons. But, again, American leadership, properly articulated, can convince them otherwise. I think that this is a mission that Europe should respond to, as well as us.

Chairman McCAIN. Senator Reed.

Senator REED. Well, thank you, Mr. Chairman.

Let me once again commend you all for the report that the Atlantic Council did. It was very thorough and very thoughtful and, I think the word continues to pop up, "timely." So, thank you very much.

General Jones, one of the recommendations was a permanent stationing of NATO forces in the Baltic. The alternative, and the one that seems to be being pursued at the moment, is a rotational force, where there would be a presence, but it would—battalions would come in and come out. Can you give an indication of what's the advantage of a permanent, versus rotational, force?

General JONES. Well, I think the permanent forces are always a little bit more expensive. I think there are really two fronts that we should consider. One is the Baltics, and the second one is the Black Sea.

I visited the—Romania recently. I was very pleased to discover that 700 U.S. marines were training on some bases that we established back in 2006. That was heartwarming; heartwarming to the Romanians, I can assure you. But, I think if the alliance decides a permanent basing is what's required, then I would absolutely support that. But, I—clearly, there has to be some presence that acts as a deterrence to Russian goals.

Senator REED. Yeah.

Ambassador Burns, your comments?

Ambassador BURNS. We support permanent stationing, because it would provide much more effective strategic deterrence against Putin. He needs to know that NATO is going to defend those countries—they're members of NATO—that article 5 will be respected. A permanent basing in the Baltics, in Poland, in my judgment, would be a much stronger warning to Putin than these persistent rotations that the NATO alliance will be announcing in the next 48 hours.

Senator REED. To every action, there's an opposite and equal reaction. That's physics as well as, sometimes, politics. So, would there be a different reaction to the Russians to a permanent, rather than rotational, force base?

Ambassador BURNS. In my view, Putin would take us more seriously if we deployed on a permanent basis, if we had installations that were permanent, if we had some capacity to defend these countries. We're not going to put, in the Baltic states and Poland, the number of troops that Putin has across the Narva River or across—in the western part of Russia. But, it has to be strong enough to get his attention, and that allows us to deal with him on a much more solid basis.

Senator REED. Ms. Smith, your comments?

Ms. SMITH. I agree with Ambassador Burns. I believe that having a permanent presence would serve as a stronger deterrent to Russian aggression. I think that Putin knows that these measures, particularly the United States measures, are temporary, and there's some question about their sustainment, from a budgetary standpoint, but just in the sheer logistical perspective, as well. I think, by putting permanent presence into the region, we do send a very strong signal to Moscow.

Now, that said, will the Russians overreact? Will they complain? Absolutely. But, they're going to do that—they're already doing that in regards to the rotational presence. I can't imagine that we'd see that much of a difference. They're complaining about Montenegro joining the alliance. I mean, the list of complaints is never-ending.

I feel like we've given Russia ample opportunity to take the so-called "exit ramp" over the last two years. He has refused to do so. I think now we need to do what we view necessary to ensure that we can defend the Baltics, should anything go terribly awry.

Senator REED. As we contemplate, and, in fact, put into effect, some of these provisions, or more constantly, the permanent or rotational force in the Baltic, talking—General Jones's suggestion of having some operations—coordinated operations in the Black Sea, my sense—or just—ask you—we also have to maintain sort of a communications channel with Russia, because one problem would be an inadvertent escalation, misreading what they're doing, and they misreading us. Is that something that you would also see as critical to—as we build up, maintaining, somehow, this effective channel of communication?

Ms. SMITH. Absolutely. Along with some of my colleagues, I ran a war game earlier this year at the Center for New American Security, called Assured Resolve, and we looked at this question of potential Russian aggression in the Baltic states, in the Nordic-Baltic region. I think the potential for a seemingly small incident to spiral out of control is considerable. Because of that, I think we do have to ensure that we have just a basic line of communication open with the Russians at all times so that we can work through a potential crisis. As you well know, they regularly, for example, fly jets, they've turned their transponders off, we've had a couple of near misses. Let's say one of those jets were to collide with a commercial airliner. We would immediately need to work that through various channels we have with the Russians.

So, yes, we have to work with them, we have to engage with them, clearly on Syria, as well, given the role that they play and the relationship they have, sadly, with President Assad. There are other challenges where we're going to need their cooperation.

So, it's challenging. I do think we can do both. I think we can build out deterrence and have a stronger deterrent inside central and eastern Europe, but I also think that we can work with them when it's in our direct interests.

Senator REED. Very brief comments, Ambassador and General, if you have them.

Ambassador BURNS. Senator Reed, the bumper sticker from— that we're going to hear in the next 48 hours from NATO is going to be "Deterrence and Dialogue with Russia." We ought to have both. I argued, in my trip to Europe, when we presented this report in Berlin and Brussels, that deterrence has to be clear and strong, and that will allow a more effective dialogue; we'll be taken more seriously. So, yes, to keep the channels open. Secretary Kerry talks to Minister Lavrov a lot.

Senator REED. A lot.

Ambassador BURNS. Many times a week. But, the Russians have to reciprocate. What Julie has pointed out, their egregious behavior towards our military, that's obviously something that's got to be brought up in that dialogue.

Senator REED. General Jones, any comments, very quickly?

General JONES. Just a brief comment to say that—following Ambassador Burns's point, that deterrence is very important. I think some in western—in the western part of Europe are more interested in dialogue and less in deterrence. But, if you go to eastern Europe, they're more interested in deterrence——

Senator REED. Than dialogue.

General JONES.—and dialogue. I think we need to focus—I mean, this is, after all, a great military alliance. I think the deterrence piece has to be—and it doesn't have to be just military deterrence. I mean, sanctions are important. economic pressures are important. We have all kinds of things that we can do, that we should do collectively.

Senator REED. Thank you very much.

Thank you.

Thank you, Mr. Chairman.

Chairman MCCAIN. Senator Inhofe.

Senator INHOFE. Thank you, Mr. Chairman.

General Jones, it's—in light of what's happened recently with our action with—in legislation that's being passed and proposed with Puerto Rico, I think it's appropriate to bring up—it's hard for me to believe that it's been 16 years since we fought, and lost, the battle of Vieques. I think it might have some—be worth revisiting today. With all the problems that they have there, I remember so well, right here in this room, with Governor Rossello, from Puerto Rico, here, talking about the fact that they were going to be closing the range. It's—and we were bluffing when we said that the Roosevelt Roads would be closed. Of course, obviously, its primary purpose was to support the live range. You remember that?

General JONES. I remember it very well.

Senator INHOFE. Do you remember also the statement you made when you were the Commandant of the Marine Corps, and you said, "Vieques provides integrated live-fire training critical to our readiness, and the failure to provide for live—for adequate live-fire training for our naval forces for forward deployment will place these forces in an unacceptable—unacceptable—high risk. Vieques must not be closed," Remember that?

General JONES. Yes, sir.

Senator INHOFE. Now that the time has gone by, I know there—there was a concern for the training that we had prior to going into Kosovo. A lot of that training, the proper training, could have taken place, but didn't. I recall also the incident where—in Kuwait, when we dropped, I think, five—three 500-—bombs off-target. That's the kind of training that maybe could have been precluded in the training in Vieques. Do you agree with that?

General JONES. Yes, sir.

Senator INHOFE. Well, the—I remember, after that, personally going to a number of places, looking for that type of training—Cape Wrath, in northern Scotland, Capo Teulada, in Sardegna, and about 15 other areas.

Now, the point that I'm bringing up is that we tried—we looked for comparable training; and, to my knowledge, we still, today, don't have the kind of training that we needed at that time. Do you think that the training that we're getting today at the various installations, instead of having it all unified in one place like we did in Vieques, is just as adequate as if we still had Vieques?

General JONES. I think the Vieques range was beneficial for not only the variety of training that we had, but also because it was on United States soil and there were far fewer caveats and restrictions. I thought it was a national asset. We—at the time, we did not—we were not able to find other areas quite to—quite like

Vieques. But, the decision was made to cease training there. It's hard to say what, exactly, the consequences of that decision were, but we certainly lost a very valuable training base.

Senator INHOFE. Well, I've been talking to a number of people there, who were on our side——

General JONES. Correct.

Senator INHOFE.—at that time, who say it could come back. We'll see what happens.

Ambassador Burns, I want to compliment you on the very strong language you used in your opening statement concerning what has happened over in the Ukraine. I and some of the others were over there during their parliamentary elections, where, for the first time in 96 years, they don't have one Communist on their Parliament. That's due to their allegiance to the West and to us. Then, of course, when Putin went in and started killing those people, our—what is your idea of our response at that time?

Ambassador BURNS. Well, I think we were—President Obama was certainly right to impose economic sanctions and to encourage the Europeans to do the same. I'm concerned, Senator, on my recent trip to Europe, week before last, that there are many European leaders—President Hollande, the Prime Minister of Italy, the Foreign Minister of Germany—who are now talking about getting to the end of those sanctions before Putin has met the letter of the two Minsk agreements that he agreed to in 2014, that he would remove his—that all forces—foreign forces would be removed, mercenaries removed, and the OSCE could deploy along the Russian-Ukrainian border. He's not—met none of those conditions.

So, there's going to be a very important discussion, slash, debate between the United States and Europe in December of this year, when the European Union has to look at whether those sanctions apply again. I think President Obama has been right to insist on those sanctions. In my testimony, I said that, in addition to sanctions, I certainly support lethal military assistance——

Senator INHOFE. Right.

Ambassador BURNS.—to Ukraine so that it can defend itself. These are defensive weapons that people have been talking about, and they——

Senator INHOFE. Well——

Ambassador BURNS.—they deserve that right.

Senator INHOFE. Yeah. Well, my feeling was, our response was totally inadequate. But, in our current defense authorization bill, as you're probably aware—as I'm sure you're aware—we are offering lethal assistance—defense assistance to Ukraine. I assume that you support that.

Ambassador BURNS. I do.

Senator INHOFE. Thank you.

Thank you, Mr. Chairman.

Chairman MCCAIN. Senator Hirono. Senator

HIRONO. Thank you, Mr. Chairman.

Ambassador Burns, you noted in your testimony that there are a number of very significant challenges facing NATO, but you saw the—one of the most significant, if not the most significant, is coming from within NATO itself, and that is this trend, what—I would call it—describe a trend toward isolationism, exemplified probably by Brexit and some comments made by presidential candidates. How would you counter this trend toward isolationism?

Ambassador BURNS. Well, that's where American leadership of the alliance is so important. We are the natural leader. We're the strongest country. The Europeans look towards us for leadership. As I said, to have one of our presidential candidates effectively denigrate the alliance, itself, threaten to walk away, I think is deeply damaging to the—to American leadership today, as it would be in the future.

Secondly, there's a lot of concern at the rightwing nationalist parties in France, in the Netherlands, in Germany, in Greece, who are arguing for isolationism, themselves, to pull back from European commitments. As we said in the last answer to Senator Inhofe, the fact that so many European politicians are now suggesting that it's time to end the sanctions on Russia, it's time to get back to business as usual—the United States can't cure all the ills of NATO. This is a debating society. We have to be convincing in our arguments. But, the American voice is very important. I'm sure that President Obama will be putting that voice forward this weekend in Warsaw. But, the next President is going to have a major opportunity to lead the alliance. As I suggested in my remarks, on Afghanistan, keeping the troops there, on defense spending, and on sanctions against Putin, there's an early 2017 agenda that we need to lead, in the United States, no matter who is elected President.

Senator HIRONO. To the other two panelists, all—well, all three of you have said that U.S. leadership is very critical to the strength of NATO. Are there other very specific actions that the United States or the President, himself or herself, should be exhibiting, diplomacy, economically, militarily, to show U.S. leadership? Very specific actions that we can take to——

Ms. SMITH. Yes.

Senator HIRONO.—show that leadership?

Ms. SMITH. I think the next President should see if he or she could convene a summit fairly early on in his or her tenure. I think a summit of NATO leaders, possibly in cooperation with EU leaders, to bring wider Europe together would be wise.

I think we have to be present more inside Europe. That will require more trips, more deploying members of the Cabinet, ensuring that we're present, that we're putting forward fresh ideas, that we're challenging the alliance, that we're asking them for leadership specifically with diplomatic initiatives, with military investments, with economic investments that they can make in the Middle East. Europe is going to be distracted for the better part of the next two years because of Brexit, again, assuming that that moves forward. But, I think the United States is going to have to push the European continent to lift its head up, focus simultaneously on the crisis at home, but also help us address the instability across the Middle East and North Africa, where it does have relationships that matter, assets that can contribute, and a lot of diplomatic heft that could be of use to the transatlantic partners, more broadly.

Senator HIRONO. General Jones, did you want to add anything to this?

General JONES. I do believe that NATO has to become a more agile organization, and it has to become more responsive the needs that are being—the threats that are coming our way, collectively.

If what we achieve is to reinvent NATO as a 20th-century defensive, reactive organization that doesn't do anything until it's too late, and then you have no choice but to fight a major war, then I think that NATO will be less useful. On the other hand, if the United States chooses to leave the alliance and convince our allies that we have—that 28 sovereign countries, working with the Arabs, in particular, who show signs of wanting to develop a NATO-like organization, we can do an awful lot to prevent future wars coming from different parts of the world, notably Africa and the Middle East.

So, I think NATO has to be more proactive. It has to be—the mission has to be to fight and win, if necessary, but also to prevent future conflicts. You can do that with 28 countries acting as one.

Senator HIRONO. I think all of you mentioned that there should be a permanent stationing of our troops. Is this going to be a subject of discussion for this Warsaw summit that's going on?

General JONES. I think it will be, yeah.

Ambassador BURNS. I think it's already clear, from the Defense Minister's meeting two weeks ago, that NATO is likely to announce, on Saturday, that it will deploy——

Senator HIRONO. Yes.

Ambassador BURNS.—rotational forces.

Senator HIRONO. Right.

Ambassador BURNS. It won't meet that permanent basis. The alliance operates on consensus, so all 28 allies have to agree. There were many countries who wanted permanent stationing, as General Jones has said, mainly the countries in eastern Europe. Some of the west European countries disagreed. So, it would be my hope that we could convince the allies to move towards permanent stationing in the next few years.

Senator HIRONO. Thank you, Mr. Chairman.

Chairman MCCAIN. Senator Ayotte.

Senator AYOTTE. I want to thank all of you for being here.

I wanted to follow up. General Jones, you had mentioned that NATO should take a more aggressive leadership role. I'd like to get to the question of what NATO's role should be, more specifically, with regard to the fight against ISIS. So, you talked, General Jones, about NATO developing a strategy—an ISIL strategy. Then I know that, in the Warsaw summit, they're going to deploy AWACS, they're also going to put some training forces into Iraq. But, what greater role could NATO play, here, because—to address ISIL? As I think about a NATO member—for example, Turkey— with what just happened in Istanbul and what needs to happen, and the operations right now on the Manbij Pocket there along the 90 kilometers along the Turkey border, where it's been a—obviously, a place where refugees have gone back and forth, and also, as we know, fighters—foreign fighters have gone back and forth, which has been very significant. I'd love to hear from each of you, Where do you think, in the ideal, NATO's role could be, along with—combined with American leadership? What should our leadership role be in encouraging NATO and the Arab nations to join together so that we can more effectively defeat ISIS?

General JONES. Senator, I think that NATO has the capacity to be very, very influential in helping Arab countries form their own version of NATO, for example. I think there's—the logic would indicate that that would be a natural mission.

First—the first obligation for NATO is to respond to its members' needs, and, where they feel threatened, that we act as one and we help in any way we can. We've done that several times, particularly with Turkey. I think we should continue to support our membership.

But, beyond that, if we really want to avoid a human disaster—another human disaster, perhaps even bigger, I think proactive engagement in different countries in Africa, North Africa in particular, but also sub-Saharan Africa, to help them form security measures that are—that enable them to defend their borders and to protect themselves, share intelligence, and collectively band together with like-minded nations to show ISIL-like organizations that they have no future and they have no hope. That involves training, it involves all kinds of development of border security, national security forces, and the deployment, I think, of NATO forces in the Mediterranean. For instance, we have unparalleled naval capabilities, and I think we need much more cohesion within the alliance to project that kind of sentiment, that NATO is not simply coming in to invade or to cause more problems, but to actually prevent problems from happening.

So, it's a whole litany of things that I think NATO—the new NATO, in the 21st century, can and should take on.

Senator AYOTTE. Ambassador?

Ambassador BURNS. Senator, I think you're right to focus on Turkey and the fight against the Islamic State in Iraq and Syria. The Turks want a closer relationship with us on issues like refugees, possible safe havens in the future, should that be possible, should this or a future administration want to go in that direction. We are also going to need NATO attention in Libya, where the Islamic State, as you well know, has an outpost. The allies are going to be critical.

The terrorist attacks in Europe have been a huge wake-up call for the European publics and their political leaders, so I think we're getting much more receptivity on counterterrorism, intelligence cooperation, judicial cooperation from the Europeans. Where I would want to see NATO act together against the Islamic State—I don't think it's going to be politically possible to have everybody, 28 countries, agree on a NATO military mission. That would help to—us to shoulder the responsibility. It would ask the Europeans to do more. They should do more, both in North Africa and the Levant. But, I don't think it's going to be politically possible to have NATO act as one, militarily, so we'll have to create these coalitions of NATO members. That's another reason why NATO is so valuable to us. Because of our joint training, we're able to work together, even in smaller coalitions.

Senator AYOTTE. Ms. Smith?

Ms. SMITH. I would love to see NATO get more engaged in the counter-ISIL coalition, in general, because I think it brings a great deal of international legitimacy. I think NATO has just incredible command-and-control assets that would be very useful. NATO also has an array of partners in the neighborhood, in the region, that it could very easily work with, as it did in its Libya operations, some time ago.

I am with Ambassador Burns. I think it is unlikely, in the short term. The debate is changing, but I don't see any major muscle movements in that regard, for a couple of reasons. One, Europe has about two million soldiers, and there are estimates that about five percent of them are actually deployable. So, there's the sheer logistics of getting there, that some of them literally don't have the forces to send and don't have the ability, if they do have the forces, to get them there. I mean, there are real capability challenges.

Two, you hear from Europeans, oftentimes, this argument that the NATO brand is too negative, that NATO's not welcome in the region. There's this mythology, in my mind, that NATO getting engaged more aggressively in the counter-ISIL mission would not be helpful. We're up against that debate. I think we could have that debate and work through it, but it is there, and it comes up quite frequently.

Then, also, I would note that NATO, as an institution, always looks for a request to get engaged. You find NATO members saying, "Well, we're—the phone's not ringing," you know, "We are not—we haven't been asked to get engaged," which is a little bit of a sad excuse. But, they do wait to be called upon to assist. They're probably hoping—well, not hoping, actually, to be truthful—that they would have a formal request come from Iraq, say, that they want NATO to take ownership of this mission, or a call from the United States, which has not come, either.

Senator AYOTTE. So, I know my time is up, but couldn't we call this——

Ms. SMITH. Of course.

Senator AYOTTE.—and say——

Ms. SMITH. Yes.

Senator AYOTTE.—"Look at what's happened—Paris, Brussels"——

Ms. SMITH. We could.

Senator AYOTTE.—"Istanbul."

Ms. SMITH. Yeah.

Senator AYOTTE. This is about all of us.

Ms. SMITH. This is back to the question about U.S. leadership. We should be asking those questions, absolutely.

Senator AYOTTE. Right.

Thank you.

Chairman McCAIN. Senator Kaine.

Senator KAINE. Thank you, Mr. Chair.

Thanks, to the witnesses.

To preface my first question, the estimate is that, at any point in time, there's about four million Americans who are either living in Europe or traveling in Europe, including 70,000 servicemembers stationed there. In your professional opinion, if the U.S. were to eliminate or dramatically reduce its support for NATO, what would the effect of that be on the risk of terrorist attacks in Europe?

General JONES. I think any diminution of American presence and leadership in Europe would cause an escalation and a probability of more terrorist attacks.

Senator KAINE. I'd like ask the other witnesses to answer the same question.

Ambassador BURNS. The Europeans depend, in large part—and we depend on them—for counterterrorism information, for intelligence-sharing, for all the things that go into that battle against terrorist groups. It doesn't all take place at NATO, but NATO's a big part of it. It's also the symbolic presence of the United States in Europe. So, it would be very detrimental.

Senator KAINE. Ms. Smith?

Ms. SMITH. Yeah, I would agree, absolutely, with both of my colleagues. I think the work that we do with our European allies, particularly in the area of law enforcement and intelligence-sharing, when it comes to addressing the terrorist threat inside Europe, it's just indispensable. I would hate to see that go away. As Ambassador Burns noted, it's not all conducted inside NATO, but there is a critical part of it that's inside the NATO alliance.

Senator KAINE. It's important to remember that the effect on Europe, which is very serious, and we should take it very seriously, is also an effect on four million Americans who are in Europe every day, including 70,000 servicemembers.

Second, in your professional opinion, what would the effect on Russian behavior be if the United States dramatically reduced or eliminated its support for NATO?

General JONES. It is Mr. Putin's ambition to weaken NATO, wherever he possibly can. I say that because I've heard him say it. I think anything that—anything that causes the United States to retreat from its presence in Europe is a good day for the Russian President.

Senator KAINE. Ambassador Burns?

Ambassador BURNS. There would be no strategic deterrence to Putin if NATO disappeared. So, from a conventional standpoint and a nuclear-weapons standpoint, NATO provides the defense of the European continent for its members against this leader, who has now divided several European countries along his southern and western border. So, it would be a disaster for Europe and the United States.

Senator KAINE. Ms. Smith?

Ms. SMITH. I think that's right. I think we'd see more military probing at sea, in the air, all over the Nordic-Baltic region and beyond. I think we'd see additional acts of intimidation, greater support for populist parties and candidates across Europe directly by the Russians. If he perceives—he already does, but if he perceives that NATO and the EU are weak and falling apart and unraveling, that will motivate him to get even more engaged in the European space. We have to do just the opposite, we have to bolster deterrence, reassure our allies, and try to send a stronger signal to him about our collective resolve.

Senator KAINE. Thank you for your candid——

Oh, General Jones.

General JONES. One other thing. We've had this discussion before, during the Bush administration, where the then-Secretary of

Defense wanted to pull troops out of Europe and—because we could always send them back. That creates vacuums. Vacuums are filled by people who don't have your best interests at heart. I think, you know, one of my favorite sayings about our presence in the globe is, " Virtual presence is actual absence." If you're actually absent, you're not influencing the—you're not—things are not going to go the way you want them to go.

Senator KAINE. Thank you for your candid answers to my two questions.

Mr. Chair.

Chairman McCAIN. Senator Shaheen.

Senator SHAHEEN. Thank you, Mr. Chairman.

Thank you all very much for the report and for your testimony this morning.

I want to begin by echoing Chairman McCain's comments and thanking you, General Jones, for your comments about what has happened at Camp Liberty. I think it's unconscionable, and I think it reflects on the United States, given the assurances that we have given. We should be doing more to address that situation. So, thank you for raising it.

You all have all referenced Brexit and the potential impact of Brexit. But, none of you have really gone into any detail about what you think will happen as a result of England's vote—or Britain's vote on leaving the EU, and how that will affect NATO, its presence in NATO, and European security. So, could I ask you—Ambassador Burns, I'll ask you to go first, if you could talk a little bit more about what you see happening as a result of that vote. The—and also maybe I could ask you about the lessons that we should be taking away from what's happened there.

Ambassador BURNS. Thank you, Senator Shaheen. Three quick points.

First, just reading the British press and talking to friends in Britain, it's not at all sure, of course, it's going to happen. We'll have to see what happens with the Labour Party and the Conservative Party and British public opinion. This may be answered in 2017 or 2018. Point one.

Point two. But, if it does happen, I think it's an ominous development for the United States, in two respects. First is, a weakened, distracted, and potentially fractured, U.K. [United Kingdom], if the Act of Union comes apart, if Scotland leaves, if Northern Ireland's constitutional position is in question, then our strongest ally in NATO—and Britain is our strongest military partner and our strongest political partner—is not going to be there for us. That's going to make it more difficult for the United States, and will weaken NATO.

Secondly, I really worry about the effect on the European Union, itself, because Britain was, and is, really our bridge to the European Union on strategic issues. Britain translates the United States to the European Union, and the EU back to us. It's a very important bridge. Without Britain's sensible, pragmatic, centrist voice—I can think of four or five instances in the last 15 or 20 years when the EU may have done something—whether it was the Clinton, Obama, or Bush administrations—that would have been vexing to us, really dissatisfying to us. So, without that role, we're going to need a stronger Germany, a stronger American link to Germany, and hopefully a stronger military power in Germany.

So, I think it's bad news for the United States, if it happens.

Senator SHAHEEN. General Jones, Ms. Smith, do either of you have anything you'd like to add to that?

General JONES. Well, I would just say, on its surface, the effect of Brexit on NATO should be marginal. The U.K. will remain a special ally of the United States and a leader in NATO. One possible effect is a more coherent EU security policy, but we'll see. Our collective prosperity is critical to our collective security. Anything that weakens the bonds of that relationship concerns me, because it will eventually erode our strength.

So, given the reality of Brexit, I think the United States should take steps to strengthen and reinforce the special relationship with the U.K. while maintaining strong ties to the EU. The United States should not be forced into choosing between the U.K. and the EU, and should use its diplomatic clout in Europe to ensure the divorce, if, in fact, it happens, doesn't destabilize Europe.

I'd just simply add that, at the NATO–EU level, there are political difficulties. There have been for the last decade. There is some reason to think that there might be some accommodations. But, part of the problem that—part of the problems that we have with NATO now is—particularly in western European countries, there's a tendency want to put a—an EU mantle on their security challenges. I just don't think they can have it both ways. It's not affordable.

Ms. SMITH. I think my colleagues are exactly right. I'll just add one point. That is the question of defense spending inside the United Kingdom. Quite recently, they were at a point where they were conducting another strategic review looking at their defense budget, as you know, and the United States pushed very hard, along with a number of other allies, but especially here in Washington, to ensure that they would maintain that two percent target.

I think, depending on how the situation unfolds, and depending on how bad the budgetary situation is inside the U.K., we could potentially see a situation where they look to the defense budget to try and find some additional resources. What we have to ensure is that that doesn't happen, that we need the U.K. to be part of the five that are now meeting that target, that hopefully will become more in the future. I would hate to lose them as the cornerstone of—in that small club of countries that are meeting that two percent target.

Senator SHAHEEN. Thank you all very much.

Chairman MCCAIN. Senator Manchin.

Senator MANCHIN. Thank you, Mr. Chairman.

Thank all of your for being here.

If I could start—and I'll start with you, Ambassador. Do you know of any experts—military experts, even retired or current military experts—that, basically, are professing that we should leave NATO, that would be advising any presidential candidate? Do you know of anybody that's setting there saying this would be a good thing, for us to leave?

Ambassador BURNS. I don't know of any experts suggesting——

[Laughter.]

Ambassador BURNS.—that we should leave NATO.

Senator MANCHIN. But, there are some military—some retired military people or Active military people that would support that?

Ambassador BURNS. I'm not aware of any.

Senator MANCHIN. You're not. Are any of you all aware? General, are you?

General JONES. I'm not aware of any that I've talked to that advocate——

Senator MANCHIN. So, we don't know where that advice would be coming—or where that counseling would be coming—that we should? Because I've been—I was at Wroclaw, at the Global Forum, and I saw the value of NATO. The thing I would—my next question—I'm going to follow up—Ms. Smith, do you know anybody that would be advocating that, that would have expertise?

Ms. SMITH. I don't.

Senator MANCHIN. Okay. So, nobody. You all should know somebody, if they were, right? I would think so.

My hardest thing was—is why we cannot—and there's no penalties that we place upon any NATO country that doesn't fulfill its obligation of a two percent—at least two percent. Some of the countries that can—when I look at Greece, all their problems, they're still committed to spending two percent. But—and I—and, I think, Ambassador, you said, about Germany, you're absolutely correct, everybody I spoke to at that Global Forum said, if Germany would take the lead, it would make such a difference in what would happen. Is there anything that we can do—the United States should do or could do—whether it's financing world global banks and all the different things that we have some strength in—could make them step to the plate? I mean, we just—we don't do anything.

Ambassador BURNS. Well, we have been fighting this battle——

Senator MANCHIN. I know.

Ambassador BURNS.—for 40 or 50 years.

Senator MANCHIN. Right.

Ambassador BURNS. I remember, the NATO minimum used to be three percent, under President Carter's administration. Now it's two percent. We've—it's gotten easier.

I do think you're right, Senator Manchin, that Germany is the key country here. We don't know what's going to happen in the German elections in 2017. But, it was very interesting to be in Berlin ten days ago to see the German Foreign Minister make these egregious comments when he said that NATO exercises on NATO territory, the Baltics and Poland, were saber-rattling. Then to see Chancellor Merkel come out, three days later, and to say she supported the NATO exercises, and she supported a German effort to get to two percent. I do think a lot will hinge on what kind of government is put together, and who leads it, in Germany in 2017. The French have elections in 2017. They're the key continental countries. If they move towards two percent, then others will move with them. If they don't, there's an excuse.

Senator MANCHIN. What I was—I've always thought that, basically, someone has to be the bad guy, someone has to be the boogeyman, if you will. If—getting into this market, this trading market and all the trading things that we do, there should be some sort of a penalty. You've got to give them a reason to go back to their electorate and says, "We have to do this, because, for us to have access to this market, this is what we have to do." Then really be strict about that. We can get people step to the plate, because I think NATO is so important to us and our success and our defense of our country. But, unless they're willing to step to the plate, the American electorate is going to get pretty tired of carrying the load we've been carrying for 40 or 50 years.

I would follow up with one other thing. I just saw where in—Putin and Obama discussing military coordination in Syria. I don't know if you saw that article yet. That they're basically—now there's coordination. It said that Putin initiated that with President Obama. Do you believe that to be a positive movement? Concrete? That something can be made out of that?

General JONES. Well, if I recall correctly, the United States has tried to achieve something like that from day one. I mean, obviously, deconflicting the airspace and reducing the possibility of——

Senator MANCHIN. What do you think brought it upon—I mean, I've read the article, here, and it's——

General JONES. Yeah. I—but, obviously, you know, if we—as you can find some accommodation, that's useful. But, I'm not terribly hopeful.

Senator MANCHIN. Ms. Smith?

Ms. SMITH. I think it's important—we both have troops on the ground—I think it's important to deconflict and ensure that our troops are not running into each other or endangering each other's lives. That said, what we have to be careful about is that Putin will make certain assumptions that this is transactional and that, by cooperating on Syria, he can get a pass on Ukraine. That cannot be part of our message. I know that the administration has been adamant in relaying that to the Russians, but I think we have to push back harder and drive that message home, both in private and at any public venue we can, so that they understand clearly that we will not trade any potential cooperation in a place like Syria for letting go on the pressure we're exerting on Russia over their actions inside Ukraine.

Senator MANCHIN. One thing I'll comment on is, our dear friends in Canada, which—Canada basically has been sliding by with Americans carrying them. They're at one percent, been at one percent for quite some time. Thirty-five States. It's the largest trading partner, with 35 States out of the 50 in the United States. That's one area that we can make a difference in extremely quickly. Do you agree, Ambassador?

Ambassador BURNS. I do. Canada has led on refugees, but they are deficient on defense spending, and we ought to be pushing the Canadians and the new Prime Minister towards a much healthier defense budget.

Senator MANCHIN. Thank you, sir.

Thank you, Mr. Chairman.

Chairman MCCAIN. Senator Nelson.

Senator NELSON. Thank you, Mr. Chairman.

When Putin moved on Crimea and used as an excuse the Russian-speaking population, it was speculated at the time that, since there's a large percentage of Russian-speaking population in the three Baltic states, especially Estonia, that he might try the same thing. What have you seen since Crimea that would indicate that he is, or is not, doing that?

Ambassador BURNS. Since Crimea, President Obama went to Tallinn, in September 2014, about four months later, and said that the security of Tallinn was equal to us, as important as is Paris or Berlin or London. That was an important statement. Now we have to follow it up with actions, thus permanent stationing of troops in Estonia, Latvia, Lithuania. Putin has not tried to cross the Narva River into Estonia. But, I would think that he would be tempted, by a hybrid offensive, to try to divide the Estonians from within, to try to play on the sympathies of the ethnic Russian population, about a quarter of the population in Estonia, even more in Latvia. That's what we've got to guard against.

We also know that Putin has been an aggressor in the cyberdomain. What NATO needs to do is build a much greater capacity to defend itself in the cyber realm and then to decide when a cyberattack does, or does not, trip article 5. This is a very difficult problem to look at, but we've got to look at. So, this is a very consequential summit coming up in Warsaw.

Senator NELSON. Couple of years ago, when I was in Lithuania, at the time, we were rotating in United States military forces into the three Baltics. Is that more on a permanent basis now?

General JONES. We—the alliance is considering permanent bases of NATO forces in the Baltics. We have—we support that in this report. Back in 2004, 2005, and 2006, we had deployments of F–16s from different countries—not just U.S., but different countries—in the Baltic states. The Russians have consistently pushed the envelope on airspace in the Baltic states. They continue to do so very aggressively. So, I don't know if that's a—an omen of things to come, but I do believe that the Russian actions over the last several years should not go unanswered. I think putting permanent troops there is a good idea.

Senator NELSON. General, from a standpoint of military warfare, if Russia really decided to move on the three Baltics, it would be very hard, because of their geographical position. So, is our deterrence simply that they know we would engage them in a fight, and that could lead to overall worldwide implications? Speak to the deterrence, please.

General JONES. Well, Senator, you're touching on a very important aspect of the alliance, and that's article 5. I think one of the things that any potential adversary needs to hear when confronting NATO is that article 5 is inviolate. I think it needs some shoring up, frankly. I think the United States President is the one who's probably most qualified and best suited to shore up whatever—to make sure there's no misunderstanding that 28 sovereign countries support article 5. That has to be heard in Moscow, and in any other place—any other capital, very, very clearly.

Senator NELSON. I agree with you. Some of the NATO alliance has been less than eager to indicate that, under all circumstances, they would support article 5. So, how do you get them to get some spine, some backbone?

General JONES. Well, I—in my view, not to repeat myself, but I think this is—if there is weakness—and I agree with you that there is at least some weakness—but, that has to be shored up critically, because the consequences for not doing that could be catastrophic.

Senator NELSON. Ambassador, how?

Ambassador BURNS. It does require American leadership. Right now, you have uncertainty in many European countries about their willingness to stand up to the Russians. We have a weakened U.K. So, for President Obama and his successor, that leadership is desired by the Europeans, and it's essential on the question that General Jones just answered. We have only invoked article 5, as you well know, once in our history. I was the American Ambassador at the time. It was the day after 9/11. The Europeans came to our defense. It was tremendously encouraging.

But, I must say, we don't see the same European unity when we talk about problems of territorial aggression in the eastern part of Europe, which gets to another point that General Jones raised earlier. We've got to be—the Americans—the champions of the east Europeans, because sometimes we don't sense that the west Europeans have the same degree of backbone that President Clinton, President Bush, and President Obama have had in standing up for them.

Senator NELSON. Thank you, Mr. Chairman.

Chairman MCCAIN. Senator Heinrich.

Senator HEINRICH. Thank you, Mr. Chair.

I want to continue, General Jones, along this line that Senator Nelson brought up of deterrence. In addition to article 5, obviously historically we have also relied very heavily on the nuclear deterrent to continue that line between eastern Europe and Russia's influence. Russia has sort of a new doctrine these days, that—this "escalate to de-escalate" approach, which I think we all find very concerning. Could you talk a little bit about how important it is that we continue ongoing modernization in that area to ensure that those assigned to the NATO mission are survivable and well exercised and ready to counter the Russian nuclear doctrine? Specifically, talk a little bit about your thoughts on this evolution to "escalate to de-escalate."

General JONES. Senator, I think that the situation is—has—that has developed is very worrisome, and it—in terms of Russia. While I do think that dialogue is important and should be maintained, I think the—what has to be shored up is the deterrence portfolio. We can do that in a number of ways. Some of the things, we're already doing. The United States is contributing monetarily to the alliance, we're contributing rotational troops, we have permanent—permanently-based troops, in a significant amount. We have the opportunity, here at the summit, for the President to make the case that the alliance is viable and is moving in the right direction for the— to meet the threats of the 21st century: missile defense, nuclear deterrent, reinvigorating the concept of article 5 in a serious discussion, given what's going on in the world. It's hard to understand that members of the alliance would not sign up to that. But, I think it's going to have to be very direct involvement at the presidential/head-of-state level to make sure that any weakness is shored up very quickly. This absolutely has to be done. Mr.——

Senator HEINRICH. Ambassador——

General JONES.—Mr. Putin has shown that he is an opportunist, and that he will take advantage of perceived weakness.

Senator HEINRICH. Yeah.

General JONES. You know, we've been through this in the Cold War, so a lot of this is, you know, dusting off the playbook.

Senator HEINRICH. Right.

General JONES. But, I also think that we should lead the alliance into more of a transformative doctrine of preventing future conflicts by acting to prevent those future conflicts and by helping others in different continents who are struggling to achieve the same kind of freedoms that we've enjoyed—developing economies, helping rule of law, teaching how militaries are subordinate to civilian leadership. All of those things, an alliance should be able to do, and it's a lot cheaper than having to fight in another war.

Senator HEINRICH. Ambassador Burns or Ms. Smith, do you have anything to add from that perspective?

Ambassador BURNS. Senator, I'd just say that transparency with the Russians is going to be really important to limit the possibility of an accidental conflict.

Second, the next administration is going to have to decide—in addition to strategic deterrence, we do need an effective—a more effective channel into the Russian Government on nuclear issues——

Senator HEINRICH. Right.

Ambassador BURNS.—and conventional-force issues in Europe. The Russians are walking away from all the agreements that we negotiated from the '80s——

Senator HEINRICH. Right.

Ambassador BURNS.—to after 9/11. It's a big concern. Getting to that is going to be an important, I think, early initiative of a new administration.

Ms. SMITH. I would just add that, before Crimea, I think the alliance, years prior, was making certain assumptions about the neighborhood—we all were—that Europe was essentially whole, free, and at peace. NATO nuclear doctrine really took a backseat in many ways, and we lost the muscle movements. We—there was atrophy.

Now what you'll see with the summit is that NATO's exercising those muscles again. It's meeting at a higher level inside the alliance on these issues. It's going to reaffirm where NATO nuclear doctrine sits in a broader deterrence policy. I don't think there'll be any major announcements tied to nuclear weapons, but I think the signal here will be, to Moscow, that NATO is in a process of reviewing where Russia stands with its own nuclear strategy, and is taking a fresh look at things like DCA, again, doctrine policy, writ large.

Senator HEINRICH. Thank you, Mr. Chair.

Chairman McCAIN. Senator Blumenthal.

Senator BLUMENTHAL. Thanks, Mr. Chairman.

Thank you, each of you, for giving us the benefit of your expertise and experience. I've been following it as I move between different committee meetings. You know how that works. I think that the focus on NATO is very well justified.

I would like to focus on what I think is a major threat to NATO's stability and effectiveness, even though it doesn't come directly from Russia. We're in the midst of the biggest refugee crisis in our lifetimes, certainly since World War II. Millions of people are continuing to flee across borders, and there is enduring chaos and violence in Syria and the wider Middle East, which, in turn, threatens the stability of Europe and, in my view, potentially the stability of NATO.

So, I'd like to ask each of you, How does the refugee crisis impact our ability to respond to Russian aggression and to maintain the strength and stability of NATO? Do you see it as a threat? If so, what should we be doing about it? Because, ultimately, if it is a threat to the effectiveness of NATO, it's something that we'll have to address before it reaches crisis proportions.

Maybe, Ms. Smith, if we could begin with you and go down the table.

Ms. SMITH. Sure. Well, thank you, Senator. Thank you for raising this issue.

The refugee crisis in Europe is transformative. It is fundamentally going to alter the face of Europe for the future. It will alter the ways in which we work with Europe. It, in many ways, in the short term, will lead to a distracted Europe and a divided Europe, because they have such wide—a huge array of differences on how to handle this crisis.

The other bad news is, it's creating a tremendous amount of friction with Turkey, one of our NATO allies, between Turkey and the European Union or other European countries. They have, as you know, managed to agree on this migration deal, and they've managed to slow some of the flow from Turkey into Greece. But, there are signs that this deal could start to fall apart and the tensions between Ankara and Brussels is considerable, and not good news for any of us.

In terms of how Putin looks at it, I mean, Putin—I think General Breedlove used the term "weaponization of refugees"—I mean, Putin has certainly realized that by putting all this pressure on Aleppo, he is potentially sending anywhere from another 500,000 to million refugees into Europe. He has opened up some of the border crossings and made it easier for refugees also to come into Europe through Finland, which is deeply troubling to our friends in Helsinki. So, he is very crafty in his use of this crisis to yield some sort of an advantage and to see how he might continue to weaken the European project.

So, in my mind, this is bad news all around. I think we have to see—since we're talking about NATO today, we have to think about ways in which NATO can play a more constructive role. NATO's already contributing to the mission in the Aegean. There's some talk about opening up that mission now to cover the waters between Libya and Italy. I think that would be wise. Not without controversy. But, I think we should challenge the alliance to think more creatively.

They're taking a fresh look at this Operation Endeavor, one of the maritime missions in the Mediterranean, and seeing how they might reshape that mission to be more helpful to deal with the refugee crisis. So, I think there's more we can do.

Certainly, I'm in a position—I believe that the United States should do more, and I think we need to figure out how we can be a stronger supporter to our European allies as they deal with this monumental crisis.

Senator BLUMENTHAL. Thank you. That's a great answer.

Ambassador Burns?

Ambassador BURNS. Senator, I agree with Julianne in all respects. I would add this. The source of the problem, of course, is Syria and Iraq—12 million Syrian homeless in a population of 22.4 million. So, at some point, we're going to have to use our influence with the Russians and the Syrian Government to get U.N. humanitarian aid corridors into those refugee areas. Number one.

Number two. I don't think we should foreclose the possibility of establishing no-flight zones and safe havens on the ground in northern Syria to protect the refugees. Turkey wants to work on that with us. Many of the Sunni Arab states want to work on it with us. Extremely complicated, dangerous. You can't—you have to plan this in a very careful way. But, if we don't do that, the refugee crisis could worsen, and therefore, the resulting impact on surrounding states—Iraq, Jordan, Lebanon, Israel possibly, certainly Europe—I think we have to face that question at some point.

Senator BLUMENTHAL. General?

General JONES. Thank you, sir.

I think Julianne said it correctly, it's a transformative threat. Right now in Europe, it's mostly handled by the European Union. But, it could easily, I think, become a NATO problem, simply because of the assets NATO can bring to the table.

But, I think that refugees from the east, as serious as it is, could actually be somewhat minor if the African continent is subverted by radicalism, organized crime, and corruption at the national levels. Refugees are caused by a loss of hope. Where there is no hope, people start moving into the areas where there is hope. Europe is the natural attraction for both—from both the east and the south. I think that this is a very serious problem. I think we should collectively address the conditions in different countries to make sure that radicalism doesn't gain the foothold that it's trying to gain, and that we continue to hold high the example of good governance and rule of law so that—you know, particularly in Africa, so the countries that are coming up for elections actually live up to their constitutions and have changes of leadership. There are some big elections coming up in Africa this year, and there are quite a few leaders who don't appear to want to step down when their time comes. That's not a good trend.

So, I think there's a lot of things that we could work on to stem a future flow that could even be worse than the one we're seeing now.

Senator BLUMENTHAL. I thank all of you for these very important insights.

I find this prospect of the continued refugee crisis and the equally alarming prospect that our adversaries will be crafty and ingenious—to use Ms. Smith's word, "crafty"—it doesn't take much craftiness to exploit this problem, but they will be, certainly, ingenious and exploitive.

So, thank you very much.

35

Thank you, Mr. Chairman.

Chairman MCCAIN. Senator King.

Senator KING. Thank you, Mr. Chairman.

General Jones, just to follow up on your final comment, I completely agree with you. I would add climate change to some of those factors, because, to the extent that the equatorial regions of the world suffer 120-degree heat, droughts, famine, that's going to motivate. I'm just afraid the refugee crisis we're seeing now is a precursor to a much more serious one caused by those regions essentially becoming uninhabitable.

Ambassador Burns, you said something very interesting. I think I picked it up. You said—talking about Brexit, you said "if it happens." Do you have information or thoughts that there may be—that the British may reverse this decision? Briefly?

Ambassador BURNS. I have no inside information, except to say I think the prevailing opinion now, two weeks—nearly two weeks later, is that there's so much uncertainty about British politics—Corbyn is—the Labour Party leader, Corbyn, is on the ropes. He's been disavowed by his members of Parliament. We'll see who wins the Conservative Party race. It could be Theresa May. She says there should be an orderly process. But, the British don't have to actually start the clock on their article 50 negotiations with the EU anytime this year. They can choose the time that they do that. There has been huge regret in the British public. You look at the capital——

Senator KING. Do you think it gets to the—my question is, though, Is there a political possibility of a reversal of the decision?

Ambassador BURNS. Some people, some political observers in London, believe that it's possible that, in 2017, a new government could engineer a second referendum. So, I don't think it's inevitable that they leave. It may be probable, but not inevitable.

Senator KING. Thank you.

Changing the subject back—getting back to NATO, I was with a group of Intelligence Committee folks in—we were in Paris the morning of the Brussels attack, meeting with French counterterrorism officials. The big lesson that we took away from that was the dreadful lack of coordination among European intelligence agencies, and their lack of—their suspicion, their lack of sharing. We then went on to Berlin. Similar situation there.

Could NATO serve as a sort of neutral repository of intelligence information that could then be shared? It—there—it just—these countries with these ancient enmities aren't going to be very cooperative with one another. Is there a Interpol or NATO—could NATO serve this function of a repository and then sharing—a kind of clearinghouse of intelligence information to bypass these silos that they now are in? Even—in Brussel—in Belgium, they have separate intelligence agencies within the country that don't talk to each other. I'm—any one of you, but—Ambassador Burns, perhaps?

Ambassador BURNS. Senator, I guess I'm skeptical. I think that NATO has never played that role in the past. There has been—there is—it's a forum to discuss issues that are outside the military and political realm, but we've never had NATO be the central repository. It would take a lot of work. All the countries would have to agree. Again, consensus is so difficult to reach, at 28. I think it's probably more likely that you're going to—you've seen, as a reaction to these attacks, greater French-German coordination, for instance; greater French-Belgian coordination. They've had to, because attacks have been transnational, across the borders. But, I'm not sure that NATO can play that particular role.

Senator KING. The problem is, if those countries aren't fully cooperative with one another, then they're only as strong as the weakest link, because you can drive from Italy to Finland.

Let me just change the subject again. The challenge with the Russians is—I think there are two—one is, you have—we've talked about how they take advantage of any weakness. The best description of Russian foreign policy I ever heard was that they were like a hotel thief who goes down the hall, trying every door until they find one that's open, and then they go in. That's really what you were saying about—any show of weakness, and they're going to try to find a way in.

On the other hand, they have a historic paranoia about the West. Frederick the Great, going back—you read Putin's speeches, and encroachment and that everybody's against them. How do we find the right balance between being protective, vis-a-vis NATO, and being provocative? In other words, adding NATO states that the Russians would view as a historic threat. Do you see the question?

General Jones, your thoughts on that question?

General JONES. Well, during our time at NATO, Ambassador Burns and I, we were actually—they were at a good time, when it looked like the NATO Russia Council was doing things. Under President Medvedev, during the first few years of the administration, we signed the START [Strategic Arms Reduction Treaty] Treaty. I actually really believed that we had turned the corner and that Russia had decided to be part of the Euro-Atlantic arc and not outside of it. But, one man changed that. I think that's to be deplored, frankly.

So, I don't know that that's going to change anytime soon. We have to recognize the situation for what it is. It is threatening. It is something that the alliance has to take under—take into account, and the 28 nations have to make sure that they send the message that some of this behavior is unacceptable, particularly if you want to avoid more problems in Georgia, in Moldova, and other places like that, that are extremely—feel extremely threatened for—by their—with regard to their future.

Senator KING. Thank you, Mr. Chairman.

Chairman McCAIN. I thank the witnesses.

Before we close, there's a story that's been banging around in the last couple of days, "Obama and Putin Speak by Phone, Ready to Increase Syria Coordination." Kremlin said, in a statement, that Putin had used the call to urge Obama to aid the separation of the, quote, "moderate opposition in Syria from the Nusra Front and other extremist groups." Who's been bombing the moderates? Is it— this stuff, you can't make up. It's staggering. It—now we're going to have a relationship with the Russians, and they're urging us to separate the moderate opposition. I wonder how many of the moderates have been killed by Russian aircraft and bombing. I just—I—it's unbelievable that we're now trying to have an accommodation with the country that has killed so many of those who we had armed and trained and equipped, and who were fighting against Bashar Assad, who is the one who has killed 250-, 300-, 400,000—I don't know, it depends on whose estimates you have—and now our only enemy is ISIS. The—and the alliance between the Iranians, Vladimir Putin, and, of course, Bashar Assad is—been solidified.

I wonder if anyone on the panel believes that, as President Obama said, it's not a matter of "whether," but "when" Bashar Assad will leave power.

General Jones?

General JONES. I'd—my personal view is, I don't see it happening in the near future.

Ambassador BURNS. He appears to be expanding his power base in Syria. We should be skeptical of any arrangement with the Russians when the Russians don't produce a diplomatic path that's real. Because the Syrian Government won't agree to it. We ought to be building up our support for the moderate rebels, our military and political support, as a counterweight. So, I would be very skeptical of this arrangement.

Chairman MCCAIN. Ms. Smith?

Ms. SMITH. I think it's shameful that Putin tried to persuade everyone that he was withdrawing from the conflict in Syria. He's not doing that at all. He's still there. He's still targeting the forces we support, and playing a very unhelpful role. I think we need to call him out on that strategy and, basically, acknowledge that he is not contributing to the future stability of the country, but, in fact, quite the contrary, continuing to contribute to its demise.

Chairman MCCAIN. I want to thank the three of you.

I also want to thank the Atlantic Council for the good work that they do.

All three of you have had great service to the Nation. I hope that—and I believe that my colleagues have gained further insight into the challenges we face, which I think we can draw the conclusion are almost unprecedented since the end of the Cold War, which makes your service and expertise and input all the more important to the United States Congress.

Jack?

Senator REED. Mr. Chairman, I simply want to second your comments, thank the panel for their work, in terms of the report and their extraordinarily insightful testimony today.

Thank you very much.

Chairman MCCAIN. This hearing is adjourned.

[Whereupon, at 11:25 a.m., the hearing was adjourned.]